Disclaimer MF

As you untie your knots, cross your t's and curve your q's. Be mindful in this MF. This workbook is not a place to wallow or rehearse old wounds. You will not be working on anyone else, just yourself. This workbook is not a place for sugar-coated checklists or empty self-promises. You're not here to pretend. You're here to transform.

Because this journey starts with self-honesty and ends with self-crowning. Take a breath homegirl, fix your lashes, and get your lip gloss; you've got work to do.

Name:

Date:

Hey Girl Hey!

EXORDIUM

There comes a moment, this moment is quiet, yet seismic. When you decide you're done handing out backstage passes to people who were never meant to be in your front row. You close the curtains, turn inward, and focus on yourself. There's no dramatic crescendo. Just a slow, steady awakening and intuitive knowing. The how the fuck did I get here moment. When you say, "I've poured enough into everyone else. Now it's my turn." This workbook is catered to assist you through that realization. Healing is not about forgetting what happened or pretending you weren't affected. It's about choosing, again and again, to prioritize your peace over your past. It's recognizing the difference between what you've been taught to tolerate and what you know you deserve.

Have you outgrown your environment but not outpaced your potential? Have you ever stayed silent or settled? Are you ready to soften your spirit and strengthen your standards? Are you bold enough to clean house and adapt to new luxurious, healthy emotions? If yes, you are in the right place.

Let's make one thing abundantly clear, you are not broken. You are becoming! This workbook will be your guide for the kind of healing that doesn't just patch you up but elevates you into the next version of yourself. You're here because something in you said, "I deserve better and now I'm ready to choose me." And baby, that voice? That's your inner healer, your higher self, and your most evolved form calling to you.

This is about being honest with yourself. Accountable every time, not just once or twice. Soft when it serves you. Unshakeable when it matters. You're not healing to revert to who you were; you're healing to meet the woman you've always been meant to become. You don't need to "start over." You need to start here. This workbook will allow you to color through chaos, feed your soul, and track your glow-up. This is not just a workbook; it is a declaration. A mirror held up to the version of you who knows better, wants more, and is finally ready to move like you are really her because you are.

Welcome, My Sweet Doll Baby

To: Be Her

Mona Graves

Instructions

1 **Go at Your Own Pace -** This is your safe space. Take your time love.

2 **Get Comfortable and Be Free** - Light a candle. Play some music. Pull out your glitter pens or highlighters. Set the vibe.

3 **Be Honest With Yourself -** No filter needed. Cry, laugh, vent. Be raw and unapologetic. Doodle all over, make it your own.

REFLECTION PROMPTS:

Purpose: To dig deep; unpack feelings, gain clarity, face your truth, and write your way through healing.

How to Use:
- Read the prompt and pause. Don't rush.
- Take a deep breath and check in with yourself emotionally.
- You don't need to finish the whole prompt in one sitting. Come back if it gets heavy.
- Let this space hold your truth... the good, the bad, and the healing-in-progress.

JOURNAL PROMPTS:

Purpose: To spark writing. Let your thoughts spill onto the page naturally and without hesitation.

How to Use:
- Read the text slowly; twice if you need to.
- Ask: "How does this speak to me?"
- Use the space to jot whatever comes to your mind
- You can bullet your thoughts or write freely.

Be FRFR

"If you can't be honest with yourself, how the fuck do you expect someone else to?"

Self-honesty is the first form of self-love. To truly accept yourself, you must recognize all parts of you: the healed and the hurting, the strong and the struggling. Stop lying to yourself and others. When people hide their true selves from others, it can lead to more damage than good. Not being honest with yourself can make you feel like someone is gas lighting you or even create a feeling of you walking on eggshells. So even if you are not the best version of yourself at the moment, always be the real, authentic version of yourself. Without authenticity and honesty, you can not address the deep-rooted issues. So please cut the bullshit with the sharpest knife in your possession, and do not write down lies.

Write about what you've been avoiding emotionally. What parts of you do you shrink, silence, or censor to make other people comfortable? What would it feel like to let that weight go?

Your Past is Not Your Prison

Your past may be a chapter, but it's not the whole damn book. Yes, you might've lingered in rooms you outgrew. Loved people who couldn't love you back. Dimmed your light just to keep the peace. But you made it. That resilience, that's your real legacy. To own your past is to face it with compassion, not condemnation. You don't need to erase what happened. You need to take the pen back and write the next chapter.

MANTRA

"I did the best I could with what I knew. I release the shame, keep the lesson, and evolve with grace. My story is mine to finish."

WRITE YOUR OWN MANTRA:

No Labels, Just Love

Take off the labels. Drop the roles. If you weren't someone's partner, mother, daughter, best friend, boss, or employee...who would you be? So many women lose themselves in what they do for others, they forget who they are within. Let this section be your pause; a moment to reconnect with the woman who existed before expectations and obligations clouded her name. And if that woman doesn't exist, think about what makes you uniquely you?

WITHOUT USING YOUR JOB TITLE, FAMILY ROLES, OR RELATIONSHIP STATUS, DESCRIBE YOURSELF IN FIVE POWERFUL SENTENCES.

1.

2.

3.

4.

5.

REFLECTION PROMPT:

Have you ever felt like you've lost yourself in the roles you take on each day? In what ways has this shown up in your life? Do you feel any resentment toward yourself or others because of it?

Temperature Check

HOT IN HERE

Think about situations that make your "emotional thermostat" run hot. These are the moments when you feel frustration, anger, or stress rising. Write down 3–4 triggers that tend to turn up your heat.

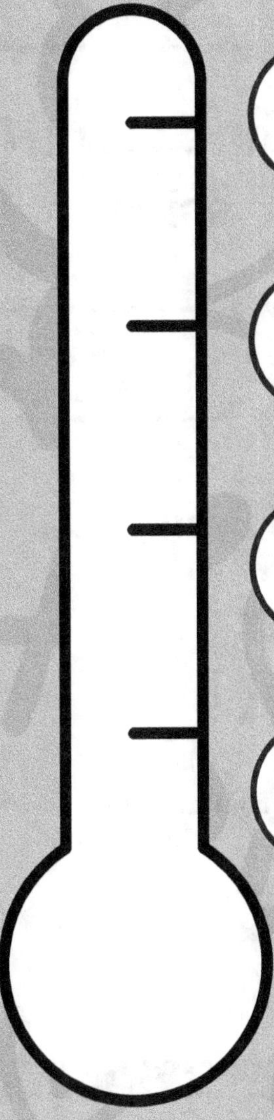

Emotional Intelligence

Emotional intelligence is more than just staying calm. It's understanding why you feel what you feel, knowing how to respond rather than react, and recognizing when to walk away while preserving your peace.

"I listen to understand, I feel to connect, and I respond with clarity and compassion."

IT'S THE ABILITY TO:

1. **Name your emotions with clarity, not confusion.**

2. **Navigate conflict without internal chaos.**

3. **Hold space for feelings without being consumed by them..**

4. **Offer empathy without abandoning yourself.**

How do you typically respond when you feel misunderstood or triggered? What would an emotionally intelligent version of that reaction look like?

Emotional Language

Most of us grow up learning just a few basic emotions: happy, sad, mad, tired. But true emotional intelligence means being able to recognize, name, and express a wide range of feelings with accuracy. This activity will help you, break free from vague emotional phrases. Explore what's really happening inside. Learn to express your emotions with power and clarity. Deepen your self-awareness and self-compassion.

Basic Phrase	What I Really Felt	Emotion Upgrade Word	Why That Word Fits
"I'm fine."	Sad and shut down	Disheartened	I felt like no one noticed how much effort I was putting in.
"I'll live."	Hurt and processing	Endured	I'm processing my pain and choosing strength despite the difficulty
"They made me mad."	Pushed to the side	Dismissed	They interrupted me and acted like my opinion didn't matter.
"Whatever, I don't care."	Let down	Deeply Disappointed	I was really hoping they'd support me, and they didn't.
"It is what it is."	Powerless and resigned	Defeated	I felt like I couldn't do anything to change the situation.

Emotional Language
continued...

Basic Phrase	What I Really Felt	Emotion Upgrade Word	Why That Word Fits
"I'm over it."	Still emotionally affected	Resentful	I told myself I moved on, but I'm still upset about how I was treated.
"I'm just tired."	Emotionally overwhelmed	Depleted	I've been taking care of everyone else and ignoring my own needs.
"I'm annoyed."	Ignored and overwhelmed	Frustrated	I had to repeat myself multiple times and no one listened.
"I'm sad."	Lonely and craving connection	Isolated	No one has reached out in days, and I feel forgotten.
"I'm done."	Pushed past my limit	Overextended	I didn't want to admit how uncertain I was feeling.

REFLECTION PROMPT:

"Think about the words you used to talk about your feelings. Did those words help other people really understand how you felt, or did they hide what you were actually feeling inside?"

My Emotional Bank: How I Withdraw and Deposit

1. GIVING YOUR ENERGY

2. GIVING YOUR TIME

3. GIVING YOUR ATTENTION

4. GIVING YOUR PATIENCE

Stephen R. Covey, in his book "The Seven Habits of Highly Effective People," introduced the concept of emotional bank accounts. The concept uses a bank account metaphor to illustrate how relationships are built through trust and positive interactions (deposits) and damaged through negative interactions (withdrawals).

Every relationship whether it is romantic, platonic, or professional; has an emotional economy. Withdrawals happen when you give energy, time, care, attention, or patience. Deposits come from joy, safety, mutual respect, and reciprocity.

Your emotional bank account tells the truth even when you don't want to admit it. If you're constantly over-drafting yourself to make others feel comfortable, it's time for a new financial model. One that prioritizes emotional wealth and protects your inner balance. The next few pages will focus on identifying withdrawals, deposits, and how to maintain a healthy emotional bank account.

Giving Your Time

Time is your most limited resource and every hour spent is a deposit or a withdrawal. Know that time is something you cannot get back. Once you feel that your time has been wasted you beat yourself up about it.

Example:

Rearranging your schedule for someone who doesn't value your time, shows up late, or doesn't show up at all.

WITHDRAW WARNING:

You keep asking yourself, "Where did my day go?"

Giving Your Energy

This is when you pour your mental, physical, or spiritual energy into someone or something that drains you in return.

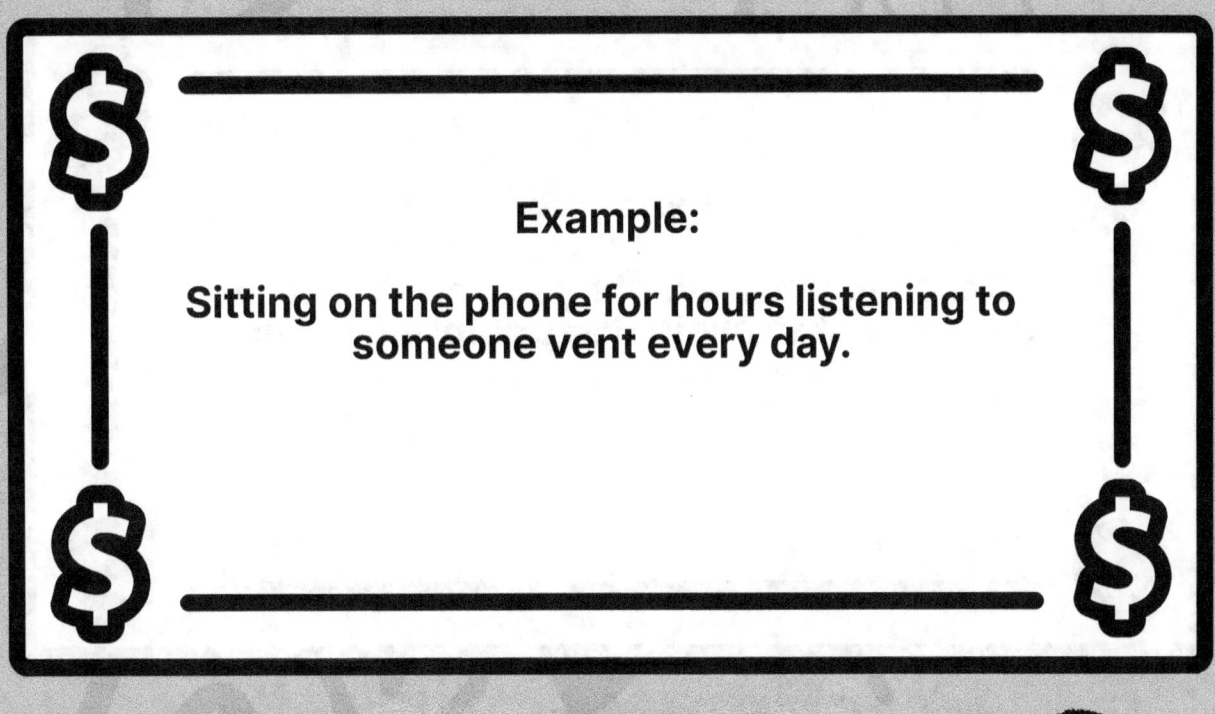

Example:

Sitting on the phone for hours listening to someone vent every day.

WITHDRAW WARNING:

You feel tired after the interaction.

Giving Your Attention

This is when you go out of your way to check in, support, or help someone who doesn't match that level of care.

Example:

Showing up to events you don't want to attend, just to avoid disappointing others.

WITHDRAW WARNING:

You feel unheard, overlooked, or emotionally starved.

Giving Your Patience

This is when you extend grace, understanding, or second chances beyond what's healthy for you.

Example:

Being overly understanding of someone's bad behavior and calling it "loyalty."

Which withdrawal shows up most often in your life, and in what ways does it appear?

What is one withdrawal you'll stop allowing this week to protect your emotional bank account?

Overdraft Notice

SUPPOSE YOU CAN RELATE TO MOST OF THE WITHDRAWALS. IF YOUR ENERGY IS LOW AND YOUR PEACE IS DISTURBED, YOUR ACCOUNT MAY BE IN THE RED. THE FOLLOWING ACTIVITY WILL HELP YOU DETERMINE HOW MUCH YOU CAN SPARE.

Emotional Wealth Tip:
Be mindful what you're saying yes to. Choose joy, safety, and respect every time because baby, overdraft fees in your spirit cost more than you think.

Cost	Emotional Expense	How It Made You Feel	Was It Worth It? (Y/N)
-50	Gave time I didn't have	Spread thin and exhausted	N
-100	Answered a 3am "wyd" text	Too accessible	N

Overdraft Notice

ADD YOUR OWN WITHDRAWALS BELOW... LIKE THE EXAMPLE YOU HAVE ONLY $200 BOUNDARY BUCKS

Cost	Emotional Expense	How It Made You Feel	Was It Worth It? (Y/N)

My Emotional Bank: How to Rebuild the Balance

Joyful Interactions

These are the people and moments that bring light to your soul.

Examples:
- Laughing so hard your stomach hurts with your bestie.
- Having deep, soulful convos that leave you feeling seen and understood.
- Enjoying peaceful silence with someone who doesn't make it awkward.

Feeling Safe & Respected

This is non-negotiable. Real deposits happen in spaces where you feel emotionally secure.

Examples:
- Being able to speak your truth without fear of backlash or judgment.
- Boundaries being honored THE FIRST TIME you set them.
- Being supported when you're not at your best, not just when you're fun or useful.

Reciprocity & Mutual Effort

A real connection doesn't feel like work. It feels natural, it flows like water in a river.

Examples:
- Someone checks on you without needing a reminder.
- You're not the only one making plans, sending love, or showing up.
- The relationship feels balanced, not like a one-way street.

Acts of Self-Care

Sometimes the most powerful deposits are the ones that you do yourself.

Examples:
- Taking yourself out, romancing yourself with no shame.
- Saying "no" without guilt.
- Logging off, staying home, and putting your peace first.
- Going to therapy, journaling, or dancing like nobody's watching.

Which areas in your life need the most work to help yourself rebuild your emotional bank account? What will the work look like for you?

Accountability

Now that you left the topic of emotional bank accounts. There is an even bigger account we need to focus on. Accountability!

ACCOUNTABILITY IN HEALING:

Accountability in healing is the personal responsibility to acknowledge your actions, choices, and patterns both the harmful and the helpful ones. While actively committing to growth, change, and emotional honesty. It means not just saying you want to heal, but showing up for that healing with integrity, consistency, and compassion for yourself and others.

Accountability is not about shame, it's about ownership.

It's asking, "How did I contribute to this?" not "Why does this always happen to me?"

It's correcting yourself when no one's watching. Apologizing without defensiveness. Making different choices because you've done the inner work. Not because someone else demanded it.

Real accountability is when you check yourself with love, not punishment. Growth doesn't always feel glamorous, but it always leads to better alignment.

Accountability

WHAT IT LOOKS LIKE IN PRACTICE:

OWNING YOUR TRIGGERS:

Instead of blaming everyone else, you pause and say, "Why did that hurt me?" You trace the wound instead of lashing out.

SITTING WITH THE HARD STUFF:

You stop running. You let yourself feel the grief, the shame, the disappointment. You don't bypass with "good vibes only" you honor the full spectrum.

APOLOGIZING WITHOUT EXCUSES:

You say, "I was wrong. I hurt you. I'm working on it." You don't use your trauma as a free pass to cause harm.

BREAKING THE PATTERN, NOT JUST NAMING IT:

You notice your toxic cycles, and then...you disrupt them. Example: You stop answering that text. You say no. You don't go back "one last time."

BEING CONSISTENT WITH YOUR HEALING:

You hold space for what happened to you, but you also reclaim the pen. You choose how the next chapters go.

Certain phrases like 'I'll try' or 'maybe' can make you less accountable. What language do you find yourself using that takes away from your accountability, and how could you reword it to take full ownership?

Write down 2 moments where you recently held yourself accountable. What did you learn from them? How good did it feel to own your shit and not place blame elsewhere?

Archetypes

Archetypes are universal patterns of behavior, emotion, and thought that reside in the collective unconscious and manifest through your stories, roles, and identity. Female archetypes in particular represent the multidimensional ways women show up in the world. Both in strength and in struggle. They are not rigid boxes, but expressions shaped by experiences, culture, trauma, and healing.

There are empowering archetypes, such as the Nurturer, the Warrior, the Visionary, and the High Priestess. These represent facets of wholeness, compassion, resilience, intuition, and wisdom. On the other end, there are shadow archetypes like the Wounded Child, the Victim, the Saboteur, or the Addict. These are not "bad," but they point to unhealed pain, unmet needs, and internalized beliefs that may distort how you relate to others and yourself.

To know your archetypes is to see your patterns with clarity. It is not about judgment. It is about recognition. When a woman identifies with the Damsel, she might begin to understand her tendency to give away her power in exchange for validation. When she recognizes the presence of the Rescuer, she may realize she is overextending herself to avoid confronting her own needs. These insights are not labels, but mirrors.

Awareness of archetypes is a profound tool in the healing process because it gives language to the silent parts of the psyche. It helps untangle the stories you inherited from survival, society, or your family. More importantly, it invites you to consciously evolve. When a woman explores her current archetype with curiosity instead of shame, she begins the process of transformation. She stops reenacting and starts rewriting.

Healing becomes possible when you know who is running the show inside of you. And once you understand your internal cast of characters, then you gain the power to shift the narrative one chapter, one archetype, one truth at a time.

Knowing the Difference

SHADOW FEMALE ARCHETYPES

Shadow archetypes represent the unconscious, wounded, or distorted expression of an inner identity. They emerge when unhealed trauma, fear, or unmet needs are left unaddressed. Shadow archetypes are not inherently evil or negative; they are simply parts of the mind and body operating from pain, survival, or avoidance. For example, the Wounded Child may manifest as hypersensitivity or emotional withdrawal, while the Saboteur might cause a woman to undermine her own success out of fear of visibility or failure.

VS

EMPOWERED FEMALE ARCHETYPE

Empowered archetypes represent the evolved, conscious, and healed self. They are guided by self-awareness, clarity, and emotional maturity. Instead of reacting from past wounds, they respond from a grounded sense of purpose and worth. They show what becomes possible when we bring light to our shadows and meet our inner chaos with compassion, structure, and self-trust.

In this activity, you'll use color not just for creativity, but as a form of emotional discovery. Each shade you choose becomes a symbolic reflection of the archetypes within you; both shadow and empowered. You may find that the darker shades reflect parts of yourself that feel hidden, overworked, or wounded; your shadow archetypes. Meanwhile, brighter or more balanced colors may represent your empowered aspects: the grounded woman, the visionary, the nurturer, the queen within. This exercise is not about making "pretty" art, it's about giving yourself permission to feel, to reveal, and to name. As you color, pay attention to your emotions, sensations, and memories. The page becomes a sacred space where your subconscious speaks in color, and your healing begins with every stroke.

THE VICTIM

CORE NEED:

To be validated, seen, and empowered.

ROOT WOUND:

Betrayal, abandonment, or abuse, especially when her voice or pain was invalidated.

BEHAVIOR PATTERNS:

- Often feels life "happens" to her
- Avoids responsibility for her emotions or actions
- May manipulate others through guilt or emotional collapse

THE SABOTEUR

CORE NEED:

To feel safe in her own success and trust that she is worthy of growth, power, and change.

ROOT WOUND:

Lack of self-trust, Fear of success, fear of change or being punished for success.

BEHAVIOR PATTERNS:

- Undermines her own goals or relationships
- Creates chaos when things are going well
- Uses procrastination, perfectionism, or crisis as distraction

THE WOUNDED CHILD

CORE NEED:

To feel nurtured, protected, and unconditionally loved.

ROOT WOUND:

Early neglect or abandonment that created beliefs of unworthiness.

BEHAVIOR PATTERNS:

- Overreacts emotionally to rejection or criticism
- Struggles with boundaries and accountability
- Emotionally immature, dependent, and has a fear of abandonment

THE WARRIOR

CORE NEED:

To feel protected without having to armor herself constantly.

ROOT WOUND:

Past experiences of betrayal taught her vulnerability leads to harm, so she armored up.

BEHAVIOR PATTERNS:

- May lead with anger, toughness, or competition
- Distrusts others and suppresses vulnerability
- Hyper-independent, aggressive, and controlling

THE RESCUER

CORE NEED:

To be loved for being, not just doing.

ROOT WOUND:

The belief that love must be earned through fixing or over giving.

BEHAVIOR PATTERNS:

- Attracts wounded partners or friends
- Ignores her own needs to "save" others
- Experiences resentment when not appreciated

THE ADDICT

CORE NEED:

To feel, process, and sit with her emotions without abandoning herself.

ROOT WOUND:

Deep emptiness, internalized shame, or chronic pain.

BEHAVIOR PATTERNS:

- Uses substances, sex, food, validation, or chaos to self-soothe
- Avoids responsibility for her emotions or actions
- Lives for the high or escape

THE DAMSEL

CORE NEED:

Empowerment and recognition of her inner strength.

ROOT WOUND:

Conditioned to believe she needs saving to be valued or worthy.

BEHAVIOR PATTERNS:

- Waits for a partner, mentor, or life event to "rescue" her
- Struggles with self-advocacy or decision-making
- Overidentifies with romanticized suffering

THE PRINCESS

CORE NEED:

To feel cherished and empowered from within rather than through external validation.

ROOT WOUND:

Overprotected or emotionally neglected; taught external beauty/status equals worth.

BEHAVIOR PATTERNS:

- Seeks validation through image, luxury, or attention
- Relies on allure or appearance rather than depth
- Entitled, superficial, avoids responsibility, or discomfort

THE HERMIT

CORE NEED:

To feel internally secure, spiritually grounded, and connected to her inner truth.

ROOT WOUND:

Fear of being misunderstood led her to isolate or hide her depth.

BEHAVIOR PATTERNS:

- Withdraws during emotional conflict
- Avoids vulnerability or social connection
- May present as mysterious or cold

THE DETECTIVE

CORE NEED:

To feel clear, discerning, and guided by intuitive truth rather than suspicion.

ROOT WOUND:

Fear of deception or betrayal that once made her overly guarded, mistrustful, or controlling.

BEHAVIOR PATTERNS:

- Constantly seeks the "truth" out of fear of deception
- Reads between every line, questions motives
- Struggles to relax or surrender control

THE VAMPIRE

CORE NEED:

To feel energized and empowered from within not through dependency.

ROOT WOUND:

Emptiness or emotional rejection caused her to drain others for attention, validation, or control.

BEHAVIOR PATTERNS:

- Thrives off chaos, attention, or emotional highs/lows
- May provoke or drain others to feel powerful or alive
- Emotional leeching, drama-feeding, and manipulation

Which shadow archetype do you resonate with most, and why?

Have you noticed more than one shadow side showing up in your thoughts, choices, or relationships? Which shadow archetypes might have been influencing you and how do they show up?

THE PHOENIX

ESSENCE:

She sees herself as the powerful author of her own life. Rather than feeling powerless or blaming others, she recognizes her ability to choose, act, and transform. She honors her past without being ruled by it. She stands in her story as both survivor and sovereign creator, rewriting old narratives with dignity and intention.

TRAITS:

The Phoenix is the healed opposite of The Victim. She embodies traits of resilience, rebirth, self-trust and ownership.

THE ALCHEMIST

ESSENCE:

She turns fear into fuel and setbacks into stepping stones. Rather than sabotaging opportunities, she leans into expansion, believing she deserves to flourish. She recognizes that every choice she makes carries sacred creative power and she refuses to play small or undermine her own blessings.

TRAITS:

The Alchemist is the healed opposite of The Saboteur. She embodies traits of transformation, mastery, and trust in self.

THE SOUL NURTURER

ESSENCE:

She has tenderly re-parented her inner child. She meets her emotional needs with compassion rather than seeking others to fill them. She moves through life grounded in self-soothing, resilience, and grace, no longer driven by abandonment fears but by self-respect and wholeness.

TRAITS:

The Soul Nurturer is the healed opposite of The Wounded Child. She embodies traits of self-nurturing, emotional maturity, and unconditional love.

THE SACRED WARRIOR

ESSENCE:

She no longer fights just to survive; she fights to protect peace, purpose, and love. Her strength is tempered by wisdom. She knows when to stand firm and when to surrender. She embodies fierce devotion without the armor of rage, trusting that true strength is rooted in love, not fear.

TRAITS:

The Sacred Warrior is the healed opposite of The Warrior. She embodies traits of disciplined strength, service through power, and peaceful protection

THE ANCHOR

ESSENCE:

She no longer saves people at the cost of herself. Through compassion without codependency, she inspires, teaches, and models growth but leaves the heavy lifting to those it belongs to. Her love liberates rather than entangles.

TRAITS:

The Anchor is the healed opposite of The Rescuer. She embodies traits of firm boundaries, empowerment of others, and healthy compassion.

THE GUIDED LIGHT

ESSENCE:

She feels her feelings deeply without being consumed by them. She seeks fullness from within, not from substances, drama, or distraction. Pleasure is sacred to her it is something she claims consciously, not something she chases to numb the pain. She knows how to self-source her joy, peace, and vitality.

TRAITS:

The Guided Light is the healed opposite of The Addict. She is led by divine clarity and deep intuition.

THE HEROINE

ESSENCE:

She is her own knight in shining armor. She acknowledges that while support is beautiful, she is not waiting for someone to save or validate her existence. She takes aligned action on her own behalf, knowing her worth is not dependent on external saviors or circumstances.

TRAITS:

The Heroine is the healed opposite of The Damsel. She embodies traits of independence, resilience, and self-advocacy.

THE QUEEN

ESSENCE:

She no longer demands adoration without contribution. She no longer chases surface level validation. She leads her life from her inner throne, embodying elegance, maturity, and power. Her worth is not measured by what she wears or how she's perceived but by the legacy she builds through her values, actions, and heart.

TRAITS:

The Queen is the healed opposite of The Princess. She embodies traits of mature self-worth, dignity, and inner wealth.

THE BUTTERFLY

ESSENCE:

She honors her need for solitude but does not hide behind it. She understands that connection requires vulnerability. She knows how to both retreat when necessary and engage authentically with others. She builds community from a place of discernment rather than fear.

TRAITS:

The Butterfly is the healed opposite of The Hermit. She embodies traits of courageous intimacy, wise discernment, and community.

THE ORACLE

ESSENCE:

She trusts her intuition without the need to obsessively verify or control. She recognizes patterns, reads energy fluently, and discerns truth but without becoming consumed by suspicion. Her power lies in trusting her gut and knowing that she can handle whatever truths unfold.

TRAITS:

The Oracle is the healed opposite of The Detective. She embodies traits of trust, clarity, and inner security.

THE RADIANT SOURCE

ESSENCE:

She does not siphon energy from others because she generates her own light. She knows how to renew herself emotionally, spiritually, and energetically. She nourishes those around her not by draining them, but by overflowing from a well of authentic joy, generosity, and presence.

TRAITS:

The Radiant Source is the healed opposite of The Vampire. She embodies traits of abundant energy, presence, and contribution.

Which empowered archetype do you want to embody right now? What habits, thoughts, or patterns are keeping you from stepping into her energy?

Switch Up the Tempo

> "Change is not the storm that comes in to drown you, it's the current that floats you to who you are becoming."

Think of a shadow archetype as the version of yourself that reacts from fear, hurt, or old habits, often without you realizing it. It's like you're running on autopilot, and those patterns keep pulling you into situations that make you feel small, powerless, or stuck. Transforming into an empowered archetype starts with noticing these patterns, even if you don't fully understand them yet. You pause, ask yourself what you really need in that moment, and choose an action that supports your well-being instead of repeating the old cycle. Over time, those small choices add up, and you begin to show up as the stronger, wiser version of yourself who acts from self-respect and clarity instead of fear.

The Victim → The Pheonix

Recognize the Pattern:	Notice where you blame others or external events for your pain.
Journal:	Journal your beliefs about powerlessness. Where did they originate?
Shift Perspective:	Reframe challenges as opportunities to reclaim your voice and deepen your understanding of who you are.
Empowerment Practice:	Set a boundary or make a decision without seeking permission. Trust your instincts and recognize that your needs are valid.
Affirmation:	"I am not what happened to me. I am what I choose to become."

Notes

The Saboteur → The Alchemist

Notice Self-Destruction:	Identify the moments when you undermine your own success or joy. Watch for negative self-talk, self-doubt, or habits that diminish your achievements.
Address the Fear:	Ask yourself, "What am I afraid might happen if I succeed?" Reflect on the fears that arise at the thought of achieving your goals.
Release:	Write down sabotaging thoughts and burn or shred them.
Build Trust:	Set small goals and follow through to rebuild your inner faith. Start with achievable tasks that boost your confidence.
Affirmation:	"I turn fear into fuel. I am ready for more."

Notes

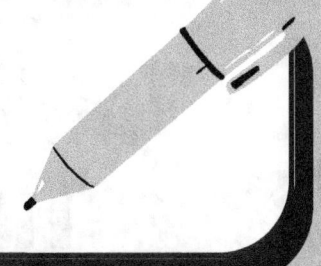

The Wounded Child → The Soul Nurturer

Meet The Little You: Visualize your inner child by noticing what she feels, and what she's trying to tell you. This will help you reconnect, heal, and nurture your true self.

Reparenting: Speak loving words to your inner child daily. Remind her of her strength, her beauty, and her worth.

Emotional Maturity: Learn to gently identify what you're feeling and offer yourself comfort and compassion, creating space between the emotion and the reaction.

Boundaries: Protect your inner child by setting clear boundaries that shield her from guilt, chaos, and emotional harm while honoring her need for safety and respect.

Affirmation: "I am the nurturing, loving presence I always needed."

Notes

The Warrior → The Sacred Warrior

Honor the Armor:	Reflect on what your anger or toughness protected you from.
Soften with Safety:	Find comfort in your own presence, in the quiet healing of nature, and in the steady support of those who truly see, hear, and honor you.
Channel the Fire:	Engage in physical movement such as dancing, walking, or stretching to release stagnant energy, clear emotional buildup and reignite your inner power.
Courage with Compassion:	Stand up for your needs and opinions, but also embrace vulnerability in environments where you feel secure.
Affirmation:	"My strength is sacred. I choose fierce love over fear."

# Notes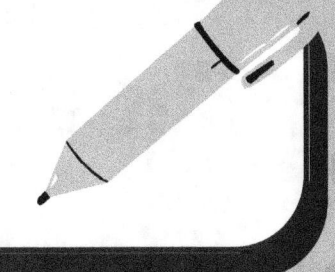

The Rescuer
→ The Anchor

Track Overgiving:	Notice when you help others to feel worthy rather than from genuine care. Awareness of this can lead to more authentic choices.
Shift from Fixing to Holding:	Practice being present with someone's pain by listening with compassion and offering support without trying to fix it.
Self-Prioritization:	Say no, even if it disappoints others, by honoring your needs, protecting your peace, and trusting that your worth isn't defined by people-pleasing.
Empower, Don't Enable:	Instead of stepping in to fix, ask, "How can I support you in doing this yourself?" to encourage empowerment, independence, and self-trust.
Affirmation:	"I guide with grace and release what isn't mine."

Notes

The Addict → The Guided Light

Identify the Escape:	What pain are you numbing or avoiding?
Come Back to the Body:	Use breathwork, movement, or grounding to reconnect.
Create New Routines:	Swap out numbness for the joy of natural pleasure. Choose to indulge in a life that rejuvenates and inspires!
Embrace Emotional Truth:	Allow yourself to fully experience each emotion without the weight of judgment.
Affirmation:	"I feel deeply. I live fully. I need nothing outside to be whole."

Notes

The Damsel → The Heroine

Spot the Savior Complex:	When do you fantasize about being saved?

Take One Brave Action:	Do one thing daily without asking for permission.

Develop Self-Reliance:	Develop new skills or make independent choices, empower yourself to trust your instincts and stand on your own.

Embrace Your True Value:	Honor your needs, set boundaries, and choose yourself even when it's uncomfortable.

Affirmation:	"Worth isn't something I earn it is something I embody, something I own, and something I never have to prove."

 # Notes

The Princess → The Queen

Check Entitlement:	Reflect on where you expect others to provide without reciprocity.
Embrace Responsibility:	Embrace your energy, take charge of your choices, and harness your desires to shape the life you truly want.
Refine with Grace:	Deepen your self-awareness, transform not only how you perceive yourself but how you engage with the world around you.
Build Inner Wealth:	Prioritize the investment in your personal growth, strengthen your character, and amplify your contributions to the world.
Affirmation:	"I lead with grace, depth, and divine authority."

Notes

The Hermit → The Butterfly

Honor the Isolation:	Understand why solitude became survival.
Slowly Re-emerge:	Take small steps. Open up with someone you trust by sharing something personal. This can be a powerful way to support your journey.
Practice Presence:	Allow yourself to be seen in real time.
Balance Solitude with Intimacy:	Create space for solitude, reflection, and meaningful connections with others.
Affirmation:	"I embrace the freedom to be fully authentic, knowing I am safe and valued in sharing my truth."

Notes

The Detective → The Oracle

Notice the Control Loop:	Track when suspicion arises and why.
Calm the Mind:	Take deep breaths, journal, or simply give yourself permission to pause. Create the space your nervous system needs to reset.
Release the Need to Know All:	Release control by surrendering to the present moment, allowing life to unfold in divine timing without forcing certainty.
Reframe your Mind:	Consciously choose empowering thoughts, challenge old beliefs, and view your experiences through the lens of growth instead of fear.
Affirmation:	"I trust myself. I release the need to control."

Notes

The Vampire → The Radiant Source

Emotional Hunger: Find the root. Where are you starved for attention or energy?

Nourishment Practices: Practice soulful daily routines that replenish your energy, restore balance, and pour love back into yourself.

Release Drama Loops: Step out of chaos and emotional spirals by choosing peace over reactivity and clarity over confusion.

Become the Light: Focus on radiating, not extracting.

Affirmation: "I generate my own joy, energy, and light."

Notes

Now that you have a few key focus points for transitioning from your shadow archetype to your empowered archetype, what are some daily actions you can take to continue showing up for yourself and strengthening that empowered version of you?

Forgiveness

"You complain about the weight on your shoulders, not realizing your hands are the ones holding it in place."

Forgiveness is an essential step in your healing because it frees you from the weight of anger and resentment. Holding onto hurt keeps old wounds alive and makes it hard to move forward. Choosing to forgive does not excuse what happened. It restores your power and emotional freedom, allowing you to acknowledge your pain and process your experiences without being trapped by suffering. Forgiveness helps you grow and find peace within yourself.

To forgive, you need to take deliberate steps. Recognize the hurt and face your feelings instead of pushing them aside. Then let go of the past and focus on your own life and growth. Redirecting your energy this way frees you from resentment and creates space for emotional balance and healing.

Forgiveness is about reclaiming your happiness and clarity. Holding onto resentment drains your energy and blocks your growth. When you forgive, you regain control of your emotions, reduce stress, and open the path to healthier relationships and inner peace. Releasing anger allows your mind and heart to experience compassion, joy, and genuine recovery.

Think about a time when someone hurt you or let you down. What would it feel like to truly forgive them? Write about what forgiveness means to you and how it could change the way you see yourself, the other person, or the situation.

First Aide

In Emotional First Aid by Guy Winch, Ph.D., the author explains that feelings like rejection, failure, guilt, loneliness, and low self-esteem can hurt you just as much as physical injuries. You probably know how to clean and bandage a cut, but very few people know how to take care of emotional pain. If you ignore these emotional wounds, they can get worse over time and start to affect your mood, your relationships, and even your physical health. Just like a cut can get infected if you leave it untreated, emotional pain can grow and make it harder for you to live your life.

Winch gives examples such as going through a breakup, losing someone you love, or failing over and over. These events naturally cause hurt feelings, but if you do not handle them the right way, they can turn into bigger problems. Emotional first aid means noticing when you are hurt inside and taking steps to heal. This might mean talking back to negative thoughts instead of believing them, or finding ways to fix a mistake instead of holding on to guilt. These small steps keep emotional pain from turning into long-term suffering.

The book makes it clear that taking care of your emotions should be just as normal as taking care of your body. Using emotional first aid helps you recover faster from life's difficulties and makes you stronger for the future. If you treat emotional pain with the same seriousness as physical pain, you can stop small problems from becoming big ones and live a healthier, more balanced life.

Failure Autopsy

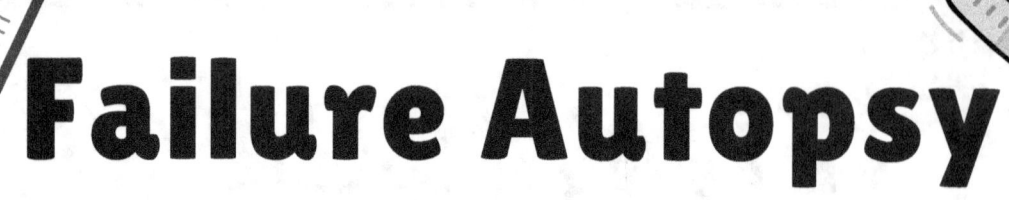

WRITE ONE OR TWO SENTENCES DESCRIBING THE FAILURE IN PLAIN TERMS.
EXAMPLE: "I APPLIED FOR THE PROMOTION AND DID NOT GET IT."

WHAT PART OF THIS WAS IN YOUR CONTROL AND WHAT WAS OUTSIDE OF IT. ASK YOURSELF WHAT YOU CAN LEARN FROM THE EXPERIENCE AND WHAT YOU MIGHT DO DIFFERENTLY IF YOU TRY AGAIN. COULD THERE BE ANOTHER WAY TO REACH THE SAME GOAL, OR IF THERE IS SOMETHING DIFFERENT THAT MIGHT BRING YOU THE SAME SENSE OF SATISFACTION.

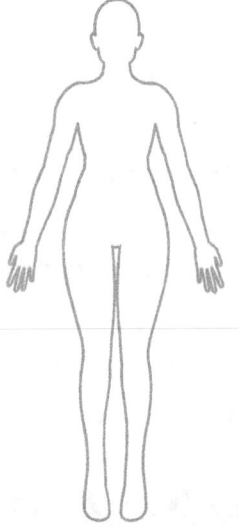

Acknowledging Patterns

"Not everything that feels familiar is safe and not everything safe feels familiar."

In The Body Keeps the Score, Dr. Bessel Van Der Kolk explains how individuals can become psychologically addicted to trauma. Trauma survivors often find themselves drawn to situations that mirror their original pain, such as chaotic relationships, risky behavior, or emotional volatility, not because they want to suffer, but because it feels familiar and oddly safe. Trauma disrupts the brain's ability to regulate emotions and sensations, keeping survivors in an unhealthy cycle. For some, high-stress environments feel normal, while peace or safety may seem foreign or even threatening.

This repetition is not just emotional, it's chemical. The body becomes conditioned to the rush of adrenaline and cortisol released during trauma, and without healing, it unconsciously seeks those same highs. The brain often prefers repetition over liberation because repetition feels predictable and controllable, while healing demands uncertainty, presence, and change.

True healing begins with awareness. It means looking at your patterns without shame and asking, "Is this still serving the woman I'm becoming?" It requires choosing short-term discomfort in exchange for long-term peace. It also means understanding that what feels like love might simply be a reenactment of survival, and real love begins when you decide to stop surviving and start choosing yourself.

What's one emotional pattern you keep repeating even though it hurts? Where did you first learn it and what did it provide you with: love, safety, or a sense of control?

Boundaries

STOP

Boundaries are not barriers; they are essential bridges that lead to healthier relationships with yourself and others. They serve as a filter for who and what can access your energy, your body, and your inner world. Remember, saying no doesn't make you unkind, it affirms your worth.

It's easy to confuse love with sacrifice or to equate strength with endurance, but boundaries teach us that love should not come at the expense of our well-being. Those who thrive on your lack of boundaries may label them as selfish or overly dramatic, but in reality, each boundary you set is an indicator of your self-worth. Maintenance of these boundaries is a daily commitment, a courageous act of saying, "Not this time" or "That doesn't work for me anymore," even when it feels uncomfortable. It's about choosing alignment over seeking approval, honoring yourself over succumbing to people-pleasing, and valuing lasting peace above chaotic comfort.

Imagine your self-worth as a luxurious meal. Is it rich, filling, and carefully made, or does it look fancy but leave you unsatisfied? What ingredients and flavors make this "meal" truly represent your value?

Peace & Non-Negotiables

"Peace is expensive. You are luxurious ."

Think of peace like your phone on Do Not Disturb mode, where nothing can interrupt your focus or drain your energy. Non-negotiables are the simple rules you establish to safeguard that peace. This could mean setting aside quiet time after work or putting your phone away during meals. These rules come into play whenever something threatens to disrupt your calm, like receiving constant messages late at night or being drawn into unnecessary drama. By adhering to these standards, you're not pushing people away; rather, you're protecting your well-being and teaching others how you expect to be treated. Prioritizing your peace is an act of self-love and respect.

Your non-negotiables are the core of your emotional hygiene. They're not "preferences." They're promises to yourself. They sound like:

- "I don't argue with disrespect."
- "I don't chase. I attract."
- "If it costs me my peace, it's too high."
- "My rest, my voice, and my time are sacred."

What does protecting your peace look like to you? What specific actions, routines, or words help you maintain peace and clarity in your life? Describe a real moment when you chose peace over drama. What did you do, say, or feel?

Essential Needs

What are your top four non-negotiables moving forward? Think about the areas in your life like sleep, work, relationships, or self-care. The areas where you need unbreakable rules. Write down four specific things that matter most to your well-being. Then explain for each:

- What is this non-negotiable?
- Why is it essential?

Example: I require respectful communication, respectful communication ensures I feel safe and valued when talking with someone. It helps others understand how to treat me well and reflects how much I value myself.

1

2

3

4

Self Care vs Self Love

Let's be real, self-care and self-love aren't the same thing, even if they sound similar. You can be doing all the self-care in the world and still treat yourself like crap. That's because self-care is what you do, while self-love is how you see yourself. And while they're different, they're deeply connected.

Self-care is all about the actions you take to support yourself. It's the bubble baths, the boundaries, the journaling, the skincare, the playlists, or the solo walks. It's anything that helps you slow down and recharge in a world that constantly demands more from you. Self-care says, "I matter, and I'm here for me."

But just because you're doing those things doesn't mean you're truly connected to yourself. That's where self-love comes in.

Self-love is about the relationship you have with yourself. It's how you speak to yourself when no one's around. It's the voice that says, "Even if I mess up, I'm still enough."

It's how you treat yourself when you're tired or struggling and how you recognize your worth without needing to earn it. Self-love is the deep, unconditional belief that you deserve rest, care, and peace simply because you exist.

Without that belief, self-care can feel empty. It becomes a checklist. You might go through the motions, but you're not actually nourishing yourself. Now flip it. If you have self-love but ignore self-care, you're left with kind thoughts but no follow-through. You say you deserve better, but you don't act like it. That disconnect adds up.

Self-love powers self-care, and self-care reflects self-love. Together, they create alignment. That is the space where your inner beliefs and your outer actions match. The goal isn't just to make them part of your routine. The goal is to embed them into your way of being, to weave them into your DNA, so that loving and caring for yourself becomes second nature.

Know Thy Self

INSTRUCTIONS: FOR EACH SITUATION, WRITE DOWN:
- WHAT YOU CAN DO TO CARE FOR YOURSELF (SELF-CARE)
- WHAT YOU CAN BELIEVE OR AFFIRM ABOUT YOURSELF (SELF-LOVE)

Life Situation	How I Can Practice Self-Care (Action)	How I Can Practice Self-Love (Belief or Mindset)
When I feel burned out		
When I experience failure or disappointment		
When I feel emotionally overwhelmed		
When I succeed or feel proud		
When I'm healing from something painful		
When I doubt myself		
When I feel tempted to return to old habits		

What I Love About Me

Using the concept of self-love, take time to write sentences that highlight the things you truly appreciate about yourself. Focus on your qualities, actions, and behaviors that make you proud or bring you joy. Begin each sentence with phrases like "I love when I..." or "I love how I..." to keep your reflections positive and intentional. This practice helps shift your mindset from self-criticism to self-acceptance by acknowledging your strengths and the moments that matter most to you. For example, you might write, "I love how I always find a way to encourage others, even when I'm having a challenging day." Aim to write at least 7 statements and read them aloud to reinforce your sense of self-worth and appreciation for who you are.

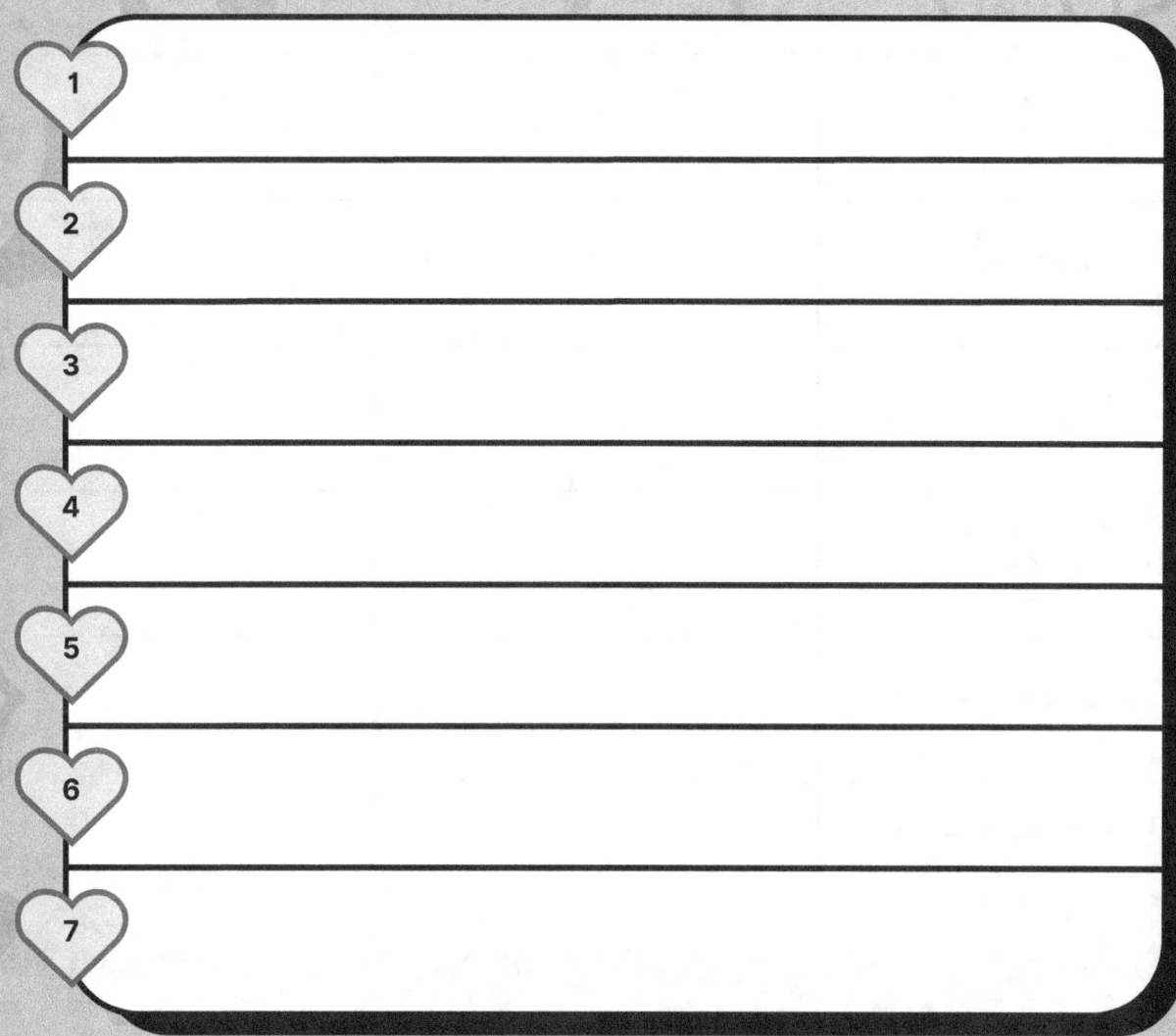

1.

2.

3.

4.

5.

6.

7.

What My Self Love Looks Like

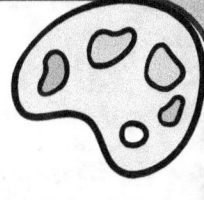

INSTRUCTIONS: IF YOUR SELF-LOVE HAD A SHAPE, COLOR, OR SYMBOL... WHAT WOULD IT LOOK LIKE RIGHT NOW? IN THE SPACE BELOW, DRAW OR DOODLE WHAT SELF-LOVE FEELS LIKE FOR YOU IN THIS MOMENT.IS IT A SOFT BLOOMING FLOWER? A HEART WRAPPED IN BANDAGES, STILL HEALING BUT BEATING STRONG? MAYBE IT'S ABSTRACT! THIS ISN'T ABOUT ARTISTIC SKILL. IT'S ABOUT CAPTURING YOUR FEELINGS IN VISUAL FORM.

A Compliment a Day Keeps the Self Doubt Away

You've been conditioned to look outside of yourself for validation. People often wait for someone else to acknowledge their beauty, brilliance, and worth. Starting today, you will make it a habit to tell yourself the truth first? This exercise is a daily practice in affirming your inner light, speaking life over yourself every single day. Because confidence doesn't come from perfection; it comes from consistent love and recognition.

Each day, gift yourself two genuine compliments. Reach deep, be bold, be resilient. Words are like seeds, so water them within yourself daily and watch your self-worth blossom.

Day 1		
Day 2		
Day 3		
Day 4		
Day 5		
Day 6		
Day 7		

The Five Disciplines

"Choosing what you want most over what you want right now."

The practice of training yourself to follow rules, maintain control over your actions, and consistently work toward your goals, even when it is difficult or when immediate desires tempt you to do otherwise. It involves self-control, focus, and the ability to delay gratification in order to achieve long-term results.

Discipline is not punishment; it's devotion. It's your commitment to building the life you want. Without discipline, confidence falters, boundaries blur, and goals slip away. With discipline, you become unshakeable. Discipline involves five key areas: mental, financial, emotional, spiritual, and physical. These are essential pillars for a balanced life. Your core beliefs define you, but these practices bring those beliefs to life. They empower you and provide freedom, rather than restriction. Each discipline shows self-respect, demonstrates inner strength, and affirms that you control your life. Embrace discipline to take charge of your path and move confidently toward the life you want.

The Disciplines

MENTAL DISCIPLINE

Mental discipline is the ability to regulate your thoughts, preventing them from controlling your actions. It means saying no to negativity, comparisons, and self-doubt while maintaining inner peace through a strong mindset. A disciplined mind reflects, re-centers, and acts with clarity.

EMOTIONAL DISCIPLINE

Emotional discipline is the ability to not suppress your emotions and more about holding space for them without letting them lead you into darkness and chaos. It's giving yourself grace while still holding yourself accountable. Allowing yourself to cry when need to cry and allowing yourself to be happy without guilt.

SPIRITUAL DISCIPLINE

Spiritual Discipline is nourishing your soul by committing to something greater than yourself, whether it's God, intuition, ancestors, or purpose. A spiritually disciplined woman is guided, not just focused on goals. She acts out of faith rather than force.

FINANCIAL DISCIPLINE

Financial discipline isn't about deprivation, it's about strategy. It means choosing long-term peace over short-term pleasure. Budgeting, saving, investing, and checking your money mindset are all essential steps toward building true financial freedom.

PHYSICAL DISCIPLINE

Your body is the vessel that holds your purpose. Physical discipline means fueling it, moving it, resting it, and listening to it. It's less about being 'snatched' and more about being sustained. You can't pour from an empty cup or a burnt-out body.

Knowing The Difference

EMOTIONAL DISCIPLINE	MENTAL DISCIPLINE
DEFINITION	**DEFINITION**
The ability to manage, regulate, and respond to your emotions in a healthy way rather than being controlled by them.	The ability to focus your thoughts, direct your attention, and control your mindset, even in the face of distractions, negative self-talk, or uncertainty.
FOCUS	**FOCUS**
• How you feel and express emotions. • Maintaining composure during emotional triggers. • Choosing thoughtful responses over impulsive reactions.	• How you think, plan, and process information. • Developing mental resilience and clarity. • Avoiding mental spirals or unproductive thoughts.
EXAMPLES	**EXAMPLES**
• Not lashing out in anger during an argument. • Staying calm under stress instead of panicking. • Practicing gratitude when you feel envious.	• Concentrating on a task despite distractions. • Replacing negative thoughts with positive affirmations. • Sticking to a decision without overthinking or second-guessing.
GOAL	**GOAL**
To stay grounded and emotionally intelligent, ensuring your feelings don't sabotage your decisions or relationships.	To build cognitive control and mental resilience, allowing you to stay productive, rational, and clear-headed.

Five Goals

INSTRUCTIONS: SET ONE BOLD, INTENTIONAL GOAL IN EACH OF THE FIVE DISCIPLINES. SETTING JUST ONE GOAL WILL GIVE YOU CLARITY AND DIRECTION WITHOUT OVERWHELMING YOU WITH TOO MANY CHANGES AT ONCE.

1.

2.

3.

4.

5.

COMMON DISTRACTIONS THAT CAN DERAIL THESE GOALS

- **Overcommitment** – Taking on too many responsibilities and losing time for your priorities.
- **Lack of Boundaries** – Saying yes to everything and everyone, leaving little time for yourself.
- **Negative Self-Talk** – Doubting your ability to stay consistent, leading to procrastination.
- **Comparison Trap** – Measuring your progress against others instead of focusing on your own growth.

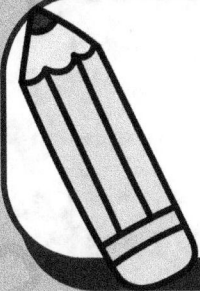

Feel Free Freewriting

THIS SPACE IS YOURS TO WRITE FREELY AND EXPRESS WHATEVER COMES TO MIND. JOT DOWN YOUR THOUGHTS, IDEAS, OR ANYTHING ELSE YOU'D LIKE.

Core Values

> "If you don't stand for something, doll baby you'll fall for anything."

If you are unsure who you are at your core or what truly matters to you, you are not alone. Many grow up without guidance on how to build a strong sense of self. Often, people make choices based on what others expect, trying to fit in or avoid conflict. This can leave you feeling confused, empty, or uncertain about your direction in life. This is where core values become essential.

Core values are the personal beliefs that define who you are and guide your decisions. They act as an internal compass, helping you make choices that feel right to you. Common values include truth, growth, respect, family, faith, creativity, kindness, and freedom. Everyone's values are unique, and they may evolve over time. The important thing is that they feel authentic to you. Discovering your values is a process of getting to know yourself. When you live according to them, your decisions reflect who you are rather than who you think you should be. You begin to attract people who respect you, set stronger boundaries, and walk away from situations that do not serve you.

To uncover your core values, reflect on moments in your life when you felt fulfilled. What were you doing, and which values were present? Consider times of frustration or disappointment and identify which values were missing. Narrow your list to the four that feel most important right now, knowing it can grow and change as you do. Your values create a blueprint for your life and a foundation to stand on. Living by them does not make life perfect, but it gives you clarity, strength, and a sense of purpose. You are not here to follow someone else's path but to create your own, and your values are where that journey begins.

Top Four Cores

INSTRUCTIONS: PICK YOUR TOP FOUR CORE VALUES. WRITE THEM DOWN AND DESCRIBE WHAT EACH ONE MEANS TO YOU IN YOUR OWN WORDS.WHY ARE THEY IMPORTANT?

1

2

3

4

Proof of Progress

"Even if no one else noticed, you did that!"

THIS ACTIVITY IS TO HELP YOU PAUSE AND WITNESS YOURSELF; TO GATHER THE EVIDENCE THAT YOU'RE EVOLVING. REFLECT ON HOW YOUR RESPONSES, BELIEFS, OR BOUNDARIES HAVE SHIFTED.

OLD ME WOULD HAVE...

BUT INSTEAD, THE NEW ME...

Write a short letter to remind yourself of how far you've come:

"Dear Me, I'm proud of you for..."

Evolution

GOAL		70%

What is evolution? Let's begin with what it is not. Evolution is not romanticizing your past. It is not clinging to the glory days, replaying old victories for validation, or measuring your worth solely by what you've already done. Too often, people pull highlights from the past instead of creating new goals, new visions, and new blueprints for the life ahead.

True evolution is the process of internal upgrading. It is the courage to admit where you are, the strength to be accountable for what you've done, and the wisdom to stop omitting the truths you owe yourself.

Evolving means making decisions from the perspective of your future self, not your old fears. It is curating your environment with intention, protecting your mind, and moving at a pace that is steady but determined. It is understanding that there is always room for improvement and embracing mistakes, both the ones from long ago and the new ones that will inevitably appear along the way.

And when shit gets hard, you meet it with more faith and more fire than it expected. You remind life that you hit harder, that you go harder, and that you will always advocate for yourself. Every single day on your evolution journey becomes a living testament to your strength, your courage, and your unwavering belief in who you are becoming.

Enviormental Factors

"You can't heal in the same environment that made you sick."

Sometimes the biggest breakthrough is not internal, it is environmental. Growth requires space, not just in your mindset but in your physical surroundings, social circles, and digital world. If your environment constantly triggers old habits, reinforces limiting beliefs, or suffocates your peace, no amount of self-work will feel sustainable. Changing your environment does not mean you are ungrateful; it means you are aware. It means you have outgrown something. And that is not a loss.

Changing your environment could be something simple, like decluttering physical spaces. For example, throwing away old trinkets, letters, and gifts from an ex. It can be finding a new job. You do not have to hate your current job, but deep down you may feel called to do something more. Changing your environment can also mean muting digital content that distorts your thoughts, or shifting routines and locations that keep you stagnant. It does not always require a dramatic move. Sometimes it is subtle but intentional. You must ask yourself: Does this space support the version of me I am becoming? If the answer is no, it is not betrayal to let go, it is protection.

Transformation thrives in supportive soil. You deserve to be rooted in environments that reflect the love, clarity, and discipline you are cultivating within yourself. Create surroundings that speak life into your goals, where your peace is respected, your growth is celebrated, and your boundaries are understood. Whether that means changing your home, your habits, or your circle, remember that you have the right to choose spaces that water your spirit instead of draining your potential.

If your environment fully reflected the person you are becoming, what would it look, sound, and feel like, and what needs to change for that to become your reality?

Identifying Toxic Environments

"Would you plant seeds in poisoned soil?"

Your environment is either supporting your healing or quietly sabotaging it in ways you may have learned to accept. When your surroundings are filled with noise, chaos, disrespect, or emotional disconnection, your nervous system stays on high alert, locking you into survival mode. Toxic environments can be obvious or subtle. They may look like people who dismiss your progress, shame your boundaries, or constantly spread negativity.

They can take the form of a friend who grows silent during your moments of celebration, a partner who becomes extremely upset when you stand ten toes down on your boundaries, or siblings and family members who make negative comments about plans or decisions you have carefully thought through. A toxic environment can also be a draining home or a digital space filled with comparison, insecurity, and dysfunctional ideals.

Even your own inner voice can create toxicity if your self-talk is harsh or unkind. Take into account that negative self talk can also be a result of the examples listed previously seeping deep down inside of you. Healing requires that you protect your peace with intention, choosing carefully what you let into your physical, mental, and emotional space. Every conversation, every habit, and every environment you step into has the power to either nurture your growth or hold it hostage. Give your family space, let the envious weird friendships go, let your partner know they can get with it or get lost. Stop planting seeds in poisoned soil.

What parts of your current environment feel emotionally heavy, draining, or unsafe and what have you been tolerating out of comfort, loyalty, or fear?

Bake A Cake

 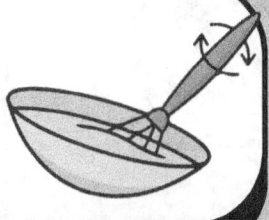

The term "I got a cake baked for that ass" simply means I am not someone or something to play with, and my get-back (revenge) is already in the oven. It may not be served right now but best believe it is baking. In this exercise, your revenge is your peace. You will be seeking peace by cutting people and things off.

In the eggs, write the name of the person, job, or thing that has brought chaos and confusion into your life. In the mixing bowl below, write all of the things they have said or done that you let slide. In the next exercise, we will bake. For now, just focus on the people or situations that have had you fucked up.

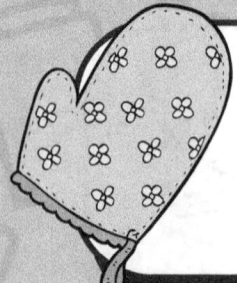
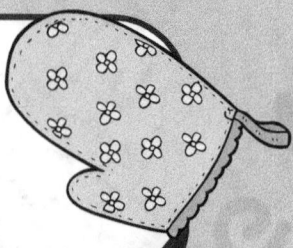

Oven Ready

WITH THE INGREDIENTS FROM YOUR MIXING BOWL, WRITTE A LETTER TO THE PERSON OR THING THAT YOU NEED TO PART WAYS WITH.

Decorate & Separate

CONGRATULATIONS!!! YOUR CAKE IS BAKED NOW ITS TIME TO DECORATE. REMEMBER THIS CAKE IS NOT FOR YOU, SO IT CAN BE AS UGLY OR BEAUTIFUL AS YOU LIKE. CHANNEL WHAT YOU ARE PARTING WAYS WITH WHILE DECORATING THIS CAKE.

Bake A Cake

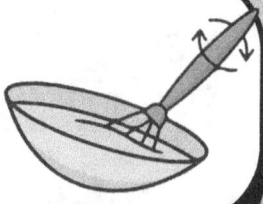

The goal is to make you a master baker. You want to master the skill of letting go of things that not only cause a disservice but frustrates, sabbatoge, and drains you. Repeat this exercise as many times as you need. Remember this cake you are baking can be a person, city, job, or situation.

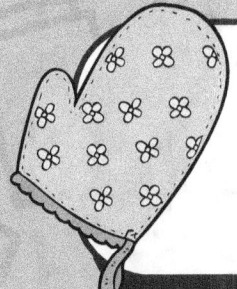
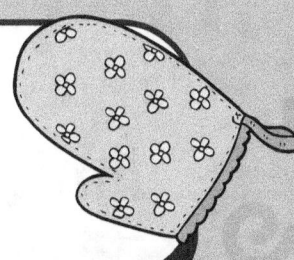

Oven Ready

WITH THE INGREDIENTS FROM YOUR MIXING BOWL, WRITTE A LETTER TO THE PERSON OR THING THAT YOU NEED TO PART WAYS WITH.

Decorate & Separate

CONGRATULATIONS!!! YOUR CAKE IS BAKED NOW ITS TIME TO DECORATE. REMEMBER THIS CAKE IS NOT FOR YOU, SO IT CAN BE AS UGLY OR BEAUTIFUL AS YOU LIKE. CHANNEL WHAT YOU ARE PARTING WAYS WITH WHILE DECORATING THIS CAKE.

What additional steps need to be taken to part ways with the cakes you baked? Focus on planning, not venting!

Soul Connection

"Your soul already knows. It's just waiting for you to catch up."

At a certain stage in your journey, affirmations are not enough. Your spirit craves authenticity and to be heard. Your soul wants to awaken your passion from within. To ignite that passion, you need to quiet the noise around you and truly listen to your inner voice, then courageously act on what it reveals. Speaking to your soul means asking, "What do I truly want?" Passion isn't always loud; sometimes, it's a whisper that tugs at you, a forgotten dream, a creative nudge, a calling you keep postponing. When you start speaking to your soul evolving doesn't feel like resisting change. It feels like embracing life.

WHAT IS YOUR SOUL PASSIONATE ABOUT?

Me, My Soul, & I

FILL IN THE BLANKS FROM YOUR HIGHEST SELF

MY SOUL LIGHTS UP WHEN I...

I LOSE TRACK OF TIME WHEN I'M...

IF I COULD DO ANYTHING WITHOUT FEAR OR LIMITS, I WOULD...

THE VERSION OF ME WHO LIVES WITH PASSION WAKES UP FEELING...

Close your eyes and inhale deeply. Turn your attention inward. Gently ask your soul the question she's been longing to hear: "What do you need from me right now?" Don't censor yourself write freely.

Brand New Brainstorm

The activities on the following pages are designed to help you clarify the new version of yourself that you are becoming. Think about how she thinks, how she moves, how she dresses, how she talks, and how she protects herself. Remember, you are not erasing the old you; instead, you are rewriting and sculpting a more polished and refined woman from the inside out.

BRAINSTORM BELOW:

FUTURE SELF

Bigger, Badder, Better

1 Her new favorite color:

2 Her top 3 qualities:

3 Her energy feels like:

4 She wears/ dresses like:

5 What does her home or personal space look like and how does it feel:

New Routines

SIMILAR TO THE PREVIOUS PAGE, DESCRIBE HER NEW ROUTINES.

Her new morning routine:

1

Her new evening/night routine:

2

What does she eat:

3

What books, podcasts, or content does she consume to expand her mind:

4

Her new hobbies/habits:

5

Start From Scratch

1 Where is she living?

What city is she in? What does her space feel like? What scents, textures, and colors surround her?

2 What does her social media look like (if she even uses it)?

What type of content does she share, consume, or avoid entirely? What energy does her online presence carry?

1 Who is in her circle?

Who does she allow close? What do her friendships feel like? How are boundaries, joy, and support flowing?

2 What does her daily environment say about her mindset?

What's in her space; books, routines, affirmations, habits? What has she removed?

Music Improvement

> "You don't need words to feel, so just listen when music speaks."

Music has a profound impact on your mood by acting as an emotional outlet. If you are feeling stressed, overwhelmed, or anxious, putting on music you enjoy can bring comfort and release tension. It can remind you of positive memories or give you the encouragement you need to keep going during a hard day. Listening to certain songs can make you feel more confident and empowered, especially as a woman, by reinforcing your sense of identity and strength.

Instrumental music, such as classical, orchestral, or jazz, can be especially helpful when you need to clear your mind. Without lyrics to focus on, your thoughts have room to slow down, and you can become more present in the moment. The flowing sounds and steady rhythms can help you relax, think more clearly, and even inspire motivation for your goals. As a woman balancing many roles, using this kind of music can create a peaceful mental space where you can recharge your energy and find fresh inspiration.

INSTRUCTIONS: ON THE NEXT PAGE DESIGN A PLAYLIST OF 9 SONGS WITHOUT LYRICS THAT YOU WILL LISTEN TO THROUGHOUT THE WEEK. EXPLORE LO-FI BEATS, CLASSICAL PIECES, JAZZ, ACOUSTIC GUITAR, OR AMBIENT SOUNDS. SPEND AT LEAST A LITTLE TIME EACH DAY WITH YOUR PLAYLIST. NOTICE HOW IT AFFECTS YOUR FOCUS, ENERGY, OR EMOTIONS.

Press Play

After listening to your new playlist throughout the week; How did different styles affect your focus, energy, or emotions? Which songs helped you feel the most calm, productive, or sparked creativity? Based on your experience, would you adjust your playlist for next week, and if so, how?

Bucket List

MAKING A NEW BUCKET LIST IS A CHANCE TO DREAM BIG AND ADD BALANCE TO YOUR LIFE. FROM TRAVEL & ADVENTURE THAT SPARKS EXCITEMENT, TO LEARNING NEW SKILLS THAT CHALLENGE THE MIND, EACH GOAL HELPS YOU GROW. YOU CAN INCLUDE PERSONAL GROWTH, BUILDING AND CONNECTION OR GIVING BACK. YOU CAN ALSO LEAVE ROOM FOR THINGS THAT ARE JUST FOR FUN, YOUR LIST BECOMES A ROADMAP FOR BOTH JOY AND PURPOSE.

Imagine you wake up tomorrow and discover you are the main character of a book. You only have one page to captivate the reader so they don't close the book. What happens in that first page, and how will you hook their attention?

My Heirloom

INSTRUCTIONS: IF YOU COULD PASS DOWN A FAMILY HEIRLOOM THAT REPRESENTS YOU, WHAT WOULD IT BE? DESCRIBE THE OBJECT IN DETAIL: ITS SHAPE, COLOR, HOW IT FEELS, AND WHY IT CONNECTS TO WHO YOU ARE. THEN, IMAGINE THE STORY THIS HEIRLOOM WOULD TELL ABOUT YOUR LIFE, YOUR VALUES, AND WHAT YOU WANT FUTURE GENERATIONS TO REMEMBER ABOUT YOU.

Imagine the new you is now a mentor, guiding others through life. What characteristics and traits do you have, and how do you inspire or support the people who look up to you?

Better Days

Create "life equations" that use simple math to show how different things add up to feelings, experiences, or moods. Write them like math problems, but instead of numbers, use words and doodles.

Examples:
Sunny days + smoothies = happiness
Homework – sleep = stress
Friends × laughter = unforgettable memories

1

2

3

4

My Weekly Planner

M		F	
T		**S**	
W		**S**	
TH			

WEEKLY PRIORITIES

CHECKLIST

- ◯
- ◯
- ◯
- ◯
- ◯

NOTES

 # Daily Gratitude

TODAY I'M GRATEFUL FOR...

MY HAPPY MEMORY OF THE DAY

TODAYS COLOR IS

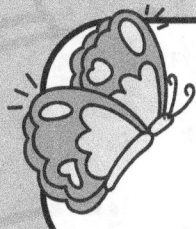

Daily Gratitude

TODAY I'M GRATEFUL FOR...

SONG OF THE DAY

SOMETHING THAT MADE ME SMILE...

Midweek Release & Renew

TAKE A DEEP BREATH AND THINK ABOUT THE PAST FEW DAYS. WRITE DOWN ANY NEGATIVE FEELINGS, FRUSTRATIONS, OR WORRIES THAT ARE STILL LINGERING.

NOW WRITE DOWN THE POSITIVE EMOTIONS OR UPLIFTING THOUGHTS YOU WANT TO WELCOME IN INSTEAD. THINK OF THE OPPOSITE OF WHAT YOU RELEASED. "I AM CHOOSING TO REPLACE THEM WITH…"

CLOSE WITH A SHORT POSITIVE STATEMENT TO CARRY THROUGH THE REST OF THE WEEK.

Daily Gratitude

DRAW A PICTURE OF SOMETHING THAT MAKES YOU FEEL HAPPY RIGHT NOW.

DESCRIBE HOW YOU WOULD FEEL IF YOU DIDN'T HAVE THIS IN YOUR LIFE, AND WHAT MAKES IT SO SPECIAL NOW.

Daily Gratitude

TODAY I'M GRATEFUL FOR...

MY HAPPY MEMORY OF THE DAY

TODAYS COLOR IS

Daily Gratitude

TODAY I'M GRATEFUL FOR...

SONG OF THE DAY

SOMETHING THAT MADE ME SMILE...

Daily Gratitude

AS YOU REFLECT ON YOUR WEEK, WHAT MOMENT STANDS OUT AS A SUCCESS OR STEP FORWARD?
THE WIN I'M MOST GRATEFUL FOR THIS WEEK IS...

AT THE END OF THE WEEK, CHOOSE A SIMPLE WAY TO SHARE YOUR GRATITUDE. YOU CAN WRITE A NOTE, SEND A QUICK MESSAGE, SAY IT IN PERSON, OR POST SOMETHING UPLIFTING ONLINE. EVEN A SHORT SENTENCE LIKE "I'M GLAD YOU'RE IN MY LIFE" CAN HAVE A BIG IMPACT.WHAT DID YOU LEARN ABOUT THE POWER OF GRATITUDE BY REACHING OUT?

My Weekly Planner

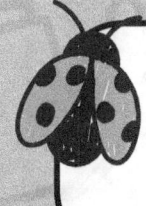

M	**F**
T	**S**
W	**S**
TH	

WEEKLY PRIORITIES

CHECKLIST

- ☐
- ☐
- ☐
- ☐
- ☐

NOTES

Daily Gratitude

TODAY I'M GRATEFUL FOR...

MY HAPPY MEMORY OF THE DAY

TODAYS COLOR IS

Daily Gratitude

TODAY I'M GRATEFUL FOR...

SONG OF THE DAY

SOMETHING THAT MADE ME SMILE...

Midweek Release & Renew

TAKE A DEEP BREATH AND THINK ABOUT THE PAST FEW DAYS. WRITE DOWN ANY NEGATIVE FEELINGS, FRUSTRATIONS, OR WORRIES THAT ARE STILL LINGERING.

NOW WRITE DOWN THE POSITIVE EMOTIONS OR UPLIFTING THOUGHTS YOU WANT TO WELCOME IN INSTEAD. THINK OF THE OPPOSITE OF WHAT YOU RELEASED. "I AM CHOOSING TO REPLACE THEM WITH…"

CLOSE WITH A SHORT POSITIVE STATEMENT TO CARRY THROUGH THE REST OF THE WEEK.

 # Daily Gratitude

DRAW A PICTURE OF SOMETHING THAT MAKES YOU FEEL HAPPY RIGHT NOW.

DESCRIBE HOW YOU WOULD FEEL IF YOU DIDN'T HAVE THIS IN YOUR LIFE, AND WHAT MAKES IT SO SPECIAL NOW.

Daily Gratitude

TODAY I'M GRATEFUL FOR...

MY HAPPY MEMORY OF THE DAY

TODAYS COLOR IS

Daily Gratitude

TODAY I'M GRATEFUL FOR...

SONG OF THE DAY

SOMETHING THAT MADE ME SMILE...

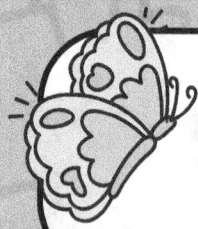

Daily Gratitude

AS YOU REFLECT ON YOUR WEEK, WHAT MOMENT STANDS OUT AS A SUCCESS OR STEP FORWARD?
THE WIN I'M MOST GRATEFUL FOR THIS WEEK IS…

AT THE END OF THE WEEK, CHOOSE A SIMPLE WAY TO SHARE YOUR GRATITUDE. YOU CAN WRITE A NOTE, SEND A QUICK MESSAGE, SAY IT IN PERSON, OR POST SOMETHING UPLIFTING ONLINE. EVEN A SHORT SENTENCE LIKE "I'M GLAD YOU'RE IN MY LIFE" CAN HAVE A BIG IMPACT.WHAT DID YOU LEARN ABOUT THE POWER OF GRATITUDE BY REACHING OUT?

My Weekly Planner

M	F
T	S
W	S
TH	

WEEKLY PRIORITIES

CHECKLIST

- ⬭
- ⬭
- ⬭
- ⬭
- ⬭

NOTES

Daily Gratitude

TODAY I'M GRATEFUL FOR...

MY HAPPY MEMORY OF THE DAY

TODAYS COLOR IS

Daily Gratitude

TODAY I'M GRATEFUL FOR...

SONG OF THE DAY

SOMETHING THAT MADE ME SMILE...

Midweek Release & Renew

TAKE A DEEP BREATH AND THINK ABOUT THE PAST FEW DAYS. WRITE DOWN ANY NEGATIVE FEELINGS, FRUSTRATIONS, OR WORRIES THAT ARE STILL LINGERING.

NOW WRITE DOWN THE POSITIVE EMOTIONS OR UPLIFTING THOUGHTS YOU WANT TO WELCOME IN INSTEAD. THINK OF THE OPPOSITE OF WHAT YOU RELEASED. "I AM CHOOSING TO REPLACE THEM WITH…"

CLOSE WITH A SHORT POSITIVE STATEMENT TO CARRY THROUGH THE REST OF THE WEEK.

 # Daily Gratitude

DRAW A PICTURE OF SOMETHING THAT MAKES YOU FEEL HAPPY RIGHT NOW.

DESCRIBE HOW YOU WOULD FEEL IF YOU DIDN'T HAVE THIS IN YOUR LIFE, AND WHAT MAKES IT SO SPECIAL NOW.

Daily Gratitude

TODAY I'M GRATEFUL FOR...

MY HAPPY MEMORY OF THE DAY

TODAYS COLOR IS

Daily Gratitude

TODAY I'M GRATEFUL FOR...

SONG OF THE DAY

SOMETHING THAT MADE ME SMILE...

Daily Gratitude

AS YOU REFLECT ON YOUR WEEK, WHAT MOMENT STANDS OUT AS A SUCCESS OR STEP FORWARD?
THE WIN I'M MOST GRATEFUL FOR THIS WEEK IS…

AT THE END OF THE WEEK, CHOOSE A SIMPLE WAY TO SHARE YOUR GRATITUDE. YOU CAN WRITE A NOTE, SEND A QUICK MESSAGE, SAY IT IN PERSON, OR POST SOMETHING UPLIFTING ONLINE. EVEN A SHORT SENTENCE LIKE "I'M GLAD YOU'RE IN MY LIFE" CAN HAVE A BIG IMPACT. WHAT DID YOU LEARN ABOUT THE POWER OF GRATITUDE BY REACHING OUT?

My Weekly Planner

M	**F**
T	**S**
W	**S**
TH	

WEEKLY PRIORITIES

CHECKLIST

- ◻
- ◻
- ◻
- ◻
- ◻

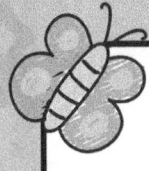

NOTES

Daily Gratitude

TODAY I'M GRATEFUL FOR...

MY HAPPY MEMORY OF THE DAY

TODAYS COLOR IS

Daily Gratitude

TODAY I'M GRATEFUL FOR...

SONG OF THE DAY

SOMETHING THAT MADE ME SMILE...

Midweek Release & Renew

TAKE A DEEP BREATH AND THINK ABOUT THE PAST FEW DAYS. WRITE DOWN ANY NEGATIVE FEELINGS, FRUSTRATIONS, OR WORRIES THAT ARE STILL LINGERING.

NOW WRITE DOWN THE POSITIVE EMOTIONS OR UPLIFTING THOUGHTS YOU WANT TO WELCOME IN INSTEAD. THINK OF THE OPPOSITE OF WHAT YOU RELEASED. "I AM CHOOSING TO REPLACE THEM WITH…"

CLOSE WITH A SHORT POSITIVE STATEMENT TO CARRY THROUGH THE REST OF THE WEEK.

Daily Gratitude

DRAW A PICTURE OF SOMETHING THAT MAKES YOU
FEEL HAPPY RIGHT NOW.

DESCRIBE HOW YOU WOULD FEEL IF YOU DIDN'T HAVE THIS IN YOUR
LIFE, AND WHAT MAKES IT SO SPECIAL NOW.

Daily Gratitude

TODAY I'M GRATEFUL FOR...

MY HAPPY MEMORY OF THE DAY

TODAYS COLOR IS

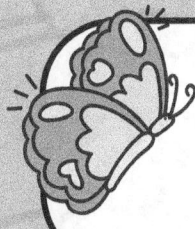

Daily Gratitude

TODAY I'M GRATEFUL FOR...

SONG OF THE DAY

SOMETHING THAT MADE ME SMILE...

Daily Gratitude

AS YOU REFLECT ON YOUR WEEK, WHAT MOMENT STANDS OUT AS A SUCCESS OR STEP FORWARD?
THE WIN I'M MOST GRATEFUL FOR THIS WEEK IS...

AT THE END OF THE WEEK, CHOOSE A SIMPLE WAY TO SHARE YOUR GRATITUDE. YOU CAN WRITE A NOTE, SEND A QUICK MESSAGE, SAY IT IN PERSON, OR POST SOMETHING UPLIFTING ONLINE. EVEN A SHORT SENTENCE LIKE "I'M GLAD YOU'RE IN MY LIFE" CAN HAVE A BIG IMPACT.WHAT DID YOU LEARN ABOUT THE POWER OF GRATITUDE BY REACHING OUT?